Communities

by
Gail Saunders-Smith

Pebble Books

an imprint of Capstone Press

Pebble Books

Pebble Books are published by Capstone Press,
151 Good Counsel Drive, P.O. Box 669, Mankato, Minnesota 56002.
www.capstonepress.com

3 4 5 6 07 06 05 04

Library of Congress Cataloging-in-Publication Data
Saunders-Smith, Gail.
   Communities/by Gail Saunders-Smith.
   p.cm.
   Includes bibliographical references and index.
   Summary: Describes various kinds of workers in a community and explains the
service which persons in each occupation provide.
   ISBN 1-56065-494-5 (hardcover)
   ISBN 0-7368-4984-X (paperback)
   1. Occupations—Juvenile literature. [1. Occupations.] I. Title.
HF5381.2.S28 1997
331.7′02—DC21   97-23589
                                                                                      CIP
                                                                                      AC

Editorial Credits
Lois Wallentine, editor; James Franklin, design; Michelle L. Norstad, photo research

Photo Credits
International Stock/Bill Stanton, cover
FPG/Michael Nelson, 4; Arthur Tilley, 6; Mike
   Malyszko, 8; Elizabeth Simpson, 12; T. Tracy, 14;
   James Blank, 1, 18; Bill Losh, 20
Unicorn Stock/Tom McCarthy, 10
Valan Photos/Andrew Farquhar, 16

Table of Contents

Police officers help us stay safe.

Doctors help us stay healthy.

Teachers help us learn.

Coaches help us play.

Veterinarians help
our pets.

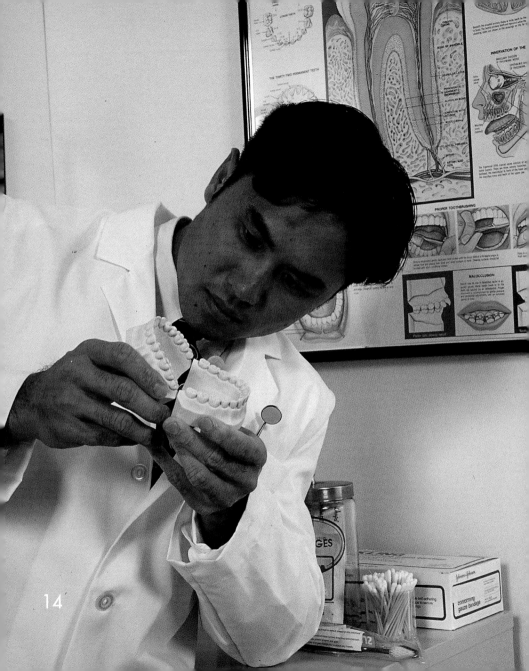

14

Dentists fix our teeth.

Fire fighters save
our homes.

625-

18

Mail carriers bring our mail.

Construction workers build our roads.

Words to Know

coach—a person who trains a sports team

construction worker—a person who builds buildings or roads

dentist—a person who is trained to examine and fix teeth

doctor—a person who is trained to help people stay healthy

fire fighter—a person who is trained to put out fires

mail carrier—a person who delivers or picks up mail

police officer—a person who is trained to make sure people obey the law

teacher—a person who is trained to show others how to do something

veterinarian—a person who is trained to treat sick and injured animals

Read More

Blevins, Wiley. *Who Am I?* Compass Point Phonics Readers. Minneapolis: Compass Point Books, 2004.

Kalman, Bobbie. *What Is a Community?* AlphaBasiCs. New York: Crabtree, 2000.

Press, Judy. *All Around Town: Exploring Your Community Through Craft Fun.* Williamson Little Hands Book: Charlotte, Vt: Williamson, 2002.

Internet Sites

FactHound offers a safe, fun way to find Internet sites related to this book.

Here's how:

1. Visit *www.facthound.com*

2. Type in this code **1560654945** or enter a search word related to this book.

3. Click on the **Fetch It** button.

FactHound will fetch the best sites for you!

Note to Parents and Teachers

This book describes people in our communities and how they help us. Each text page begins with a plural noun. The noun change is clearly illustrated in each photo. The limited repetition in the remainder of the sentence may call for teacher or parent support for beginning readers. The pronouns "us" and "our" are both used. Children may need assistance in using the Table of Contents, Words to Know, Read More, Internet Sites, and Index sections of the book.

Index

Word Count: 42
Early-Intervention Level: 7